THE POP MUSIC BUSINESS

Philip Hayward

The Media

Advertising
Book Publishing
Cinema
Magazines
The Pop Music Business
Newspapers
Radio
Television and Video

Series designer: David Armitage
Editor: Tim Byrne
Designer: Ross George

Cover: *Madonna, seen here live in concert, is one of
the most successful female singers of all time.*

First published in 1988 by
Wayland (Publishers) Ltd
61 Western Road, Hove
East Sussex BN3 1JD, England

Phototypeset by Oliver Dawkins, Burgess Hill,
West Sussex, England
Printed in Italy by G. Canale & C.S.p.A., Turin
Bound in France by AGM

British Library Cataloguing in Publication Data

Hayward, Philip
   The Pop music business. — (The Media)
   1. Pop music industries. For children
   I. Title   II. Series
   338.4'778042
   ISBN 1−85210−288−8

Contents

1 The record industry

Music is one of the oldest forms of entertainment. Its roots go back to the sounds our ancient ancestors made long before the development of spoken language. Early people made the first basic musical instruments, such as pipes and drums, and over thousands of years developed them into the kind of sophisticated instruments we have today. But even though music stretches back this far, up until 100 years ago the only way to actually *hear* music was to be present at a live performance.

Live musical performances are still very popular, but the biggest breakthrough for modern music has been the ability to record sound and to play it back in our homes, cars or public places. This has made music available on a wider scale than ever before and it is now an important everyday feature of our personal and social lives.

Sound recording began as early as 1877 when the American inventor Thomas Edison designed and built a machine called a phonograph. This device worked in much the same way as a modern record player, with a needle running along a groove, but instead of

The Eurythmics have exploited the full range of modern recording technology and are a highly popular live act.

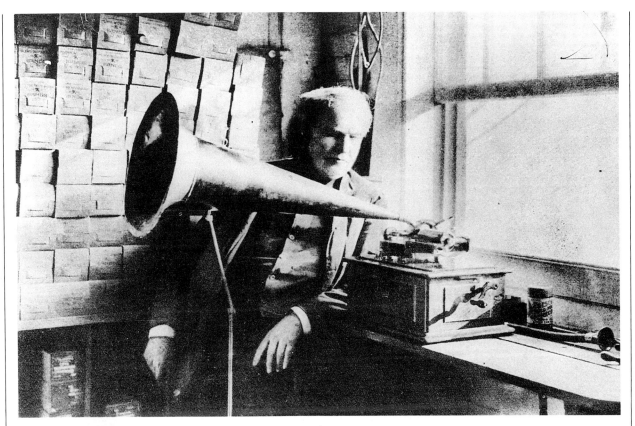

the groove being cut into a flat disc, it was on the outside of a hollow tube. These machines were first used in offices to record messages but proved both unreliable and unpopular with staff. By 1890 phonograph sales were declining and it was not until a manufacturing manager called Louis Glass discovered the idea of using the phonograph as a means of entertainment that sales began to rise.

Glass set up a number of rooms full of phonograph machines across the USA and charged members of the public a small fee to listen to short cylinder recordings. These places (known as 'phonograph parlours') quickly became popular, and the phonograph companies paid musicians and comedians to make recordings of their acts to play to the public. By 1894 the phonograph was such a popular device that manufacturers began to make small portable phonographs for home use. While portable phonographs opened up new markets for the industry, it was not until the introduction of the current disc playing gramophones in the late 1890s that the foundations of today's recording industry were established.

Thomas Edison, inventor of the phonograph, which preceded today's record, cassette and CD systems.

By the time of the outbreak of the First World War in 1914, the gramophone was established as a standard item in the homes of all but the poorest people. A number of singers and musicians rapidly became stars and their latest recordings were eagerly bought by fans, with a fraction of the cost of each record going to the performers themselves (the sum known as a 'royalty'). Up until the mid 1920s the recording industry continued to do well, as it was the only form of ready-made home entertainment, but a new competitor soon threatened their large profits.

The new competitor was radio. Radio technology had developed rapidly during the First World War and by the mid 1920s radio broadcasting stations began to be set up in Europe and North America. In countries such as Britain, radio stations, closely supervised by governments, broadcast a carefully chosen selection of talks, plays and classical music. In countries such as the USA they were set up on a very different basis.

A family in the 1930s would spend an evening listening to the radio. This was before the days of television and home video.

Radio stations in the USA were set up to make a profit for their owners and therefore tried to provide the public with just the sort of popular music and entertainment they wanted to hear. They were immediately popular, not only for their choice of programmes but also for their good quality sound (which was far better than the muffled tones of early gramophones). The popularity of radio lost the US recording industry a lot of its former customers, and even the introduction of new devices such as jukeboxes could not stop the companies' income falling by 75 per cent between 1929 and 1931. The situation worsened until the mid 1930s. Then the worldwide Depression ended and the industry slowly began to recover.

During the hardships of the Second World War people turned increasingly to music as a form of entertainment. British radio began to play more popular music to keep morale up in the factories and armed forces. But the industry obviously had to take second place to the needs of war production and did not have a chance to expand until after the war ended in 1945.

The big breakthrough for the industry came with the introduction of a new format of disc, the long-playing record (or LP as it became known). The LP was a new low cost 12-inch diameter record, which revolved at the slow speed of 33 revolutions per minute (rpm) and could therefore contain more music than the other types of disc available which revolved at speeds of 45 and 78 rpm. For a while these three different formats competed with each other, but eventually the 78 rpm record dropped out of use. From the 1950s onwards two formats became established: 12-inch diameter LP records and 7-inch 45 rpm records, which carried a single track on each side (and therefore became known as 'singles').

Up until the 1950s the recording industry was dominated by a small number of major companies who released classical or mass popularity records on a small number of their own labels, but the introduction of the LP resulted in significant changes. The new cheap LP format meant that many of the small specialist labels who had been releasing jazz, blues and gospel music and struggling by on low profits since the early 1940s could begin to make more money. Many new specialist labels were also set up to join them and not only succeeded in popularizing jazz and blues music in the USA, but also spread its influence across the Atlantic to Britain and Europe, where a growing generation began to listen to a whole new range of music. The arrival of rock and roll in the 1950s provided a further boost to the record industry in the USA and Europe. It introduced young people to a new exciting style of music that paved the way for the pop music explosion of the next decade.

Right *Blues star Billie Holiday became popular in the 1940s as new record labels brought different types of music to a mass audience.*

Below *In the 1950s Elvis Presley introduced the new style of rock and roll to young people. As a result the record industry expanded as sales increased.*

In the 1960s, the massive popularity of bands like the Beatles and the Rolling Stones and Tamla Motown acts such as the Supremes and The Four Tops, brought a fresh source of profits to the record companies through sales of both singles and albums. At the same time a new development in popular music sales occurred. A number of new groups sold large amounts of LPs without having any hit singles. During the 1970s so called 'progressive' rock groups such as Pink Floyd and Led Zeppelin and musicians such as Mike Oldfield became major stars on this basis. However, pop bands like ABBA continued to sell massive quantities of singles.

By the late 1970s the form of dance music known as 'disco' became increasingly popular and its sales combined with continuing pop and rock sales to make 1978 a boom year for the recording industry. Massive sales of records such as the film soundtracks of *Saturday Night*

Above   *The Beatles started out in Liverpool, England in the early 1960s, and went on to become one of the most successful groups ever.*

Right   *ABBA, a major international act in the 1970s, sold 220 million records worldwide at a time when sales in general were falling.*

Fever and *Grease* resulted in the US industry selling 4.2 billion dollars' worth of records and tapes in 1978 alone. But over the next five years, the international record industry profits fell drastically. This was partly due to a decline in the economies of North American and Western European countries, but also due to a new factor, a reduction in sales brought about by people 'home taping' — making cassette copies of records they would have otherwise gone out and bought.

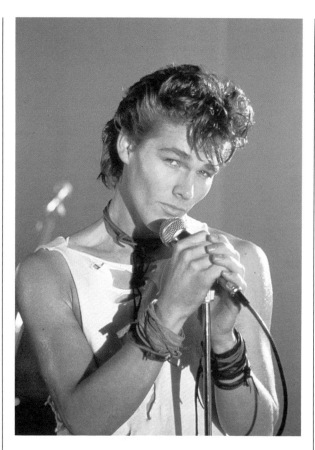

Cassette tapes were first introduced in the late 1960s to replace the old 'reel to reel' tapes. They offered an alternative to records that was easier to use in, for example, cars and social venues. At first, cassette machines were seen as a lower quality alternative to record players, but as new forms of playback machines, such as the large and powerful 'ghetto blasters' and personal hi-fis became popular, cassette sales soared. Indeed, since 1983 the recording industry has sold as many individual cassettes as discs.

Along with sales of pre-recorded cassettes, sales of blank tapes also boomed from the mid 1970s onwards as home taping became increasingly popular. By the early 1980s this practice was so widespread that a survey in the USA estimated that record companies were losing $1.5 billion annually through home taping. In order to try to get some of this lost revenue back, the industry has continually exerted pressure on governments to charge a levy (a set fee) on the sales of all blank audio-cassettes, which would go back to the record companies to replace their lost revenues.

Above   *Chart topping band Aha sold more copies of their album* Hunting High and Low *on cassette than on vinyl.*

Below   *Although a millionaire, it is estimated that Elton John loses a great deal of money through illegal home-taping of his records.*

Surprisingly, although home taping has continued, the industry has actually increased its profitability since 1983. This has been brought about as a result of the introduction of new format discs such as the expensively priced 12-inch singles, new 'mid price' ranges of albums, special cassette compilations and the successful introduction of the latest recording format, the compact disc (CD).

The CD is the latest and most sophisticated form of sound playback technology. Introduced to the market in 1983 the CD has now become commercially very successful. The disc itself is a small plastic object measuring 12 cm (just under 5ins) in diameter. Instead of playing the disc with a needle like a normal record player

The compact disc (CD), with its high quality sound, has replaced vinyl records and cassettes as the latest development in playback technology.

the CD player projects a tiny laser beam into the grooves. The music on the disc is recorded electronically (digitally) and produces a high quality sound which does not deteriorate unless the disc itself is damaged — throughout its life, it sounds just as good as it did the first time it was played. Given its high quality and the continued drop in price as it becomes more established, it could eventually replace the old easily damaged vinyl disc completely. In the short term CD technology has provided a new boost for the recording industry.

2 How the industry works

Though there are a large number of individual record companies spread throughout the world, the international recording industry is dominated by a small group of major multi-national companies. The five largest of these are CBS (Columbia Broadcasting Systems), WEA (Warner Brothers-Electric-Atlantic), EMI (Electrical and Musical Industries), Polygram and BMG (Bertlesmann Group). Between them they earned $5,000 million through business in 1986 alone. These companies are highly profitable operations which are run to make the maximum profits for their owners.
Consequently the music their artists record is treated as a 'product', which has to be carefully marketed to sell as many copies as possible.

These companies are organized into a number of separate departments which deal with the various stages of record production and marketing. This organization has remained basically the same since the early days of the industry.

One of the most important sections of a successful record company is its A & R (artist and repertoire) department. The A & R department deals with the relations between the record company and the artists who record for it. The department acts as a 'talent scout' for the label, looking for new acts to sign up and also works with the artists on the label to ensure everything goes smoothly.

The term 'artist and repertoire' is derived from the days when record companies used to control the artists on their label, choosing songs for them to record, selecting backing musicians

Artists such as Michael Jackson generate big business for record companies. His album Thriller *produced huge profits for the company.*

In the recording studios producers are backed up by a team of engineers. Artists go to a studio to record their music and the producer mixes all the sounds together into the final product.

and producers and deciding which records should be released and when. In the early days only the best selling artists could influence the record companies decisions on these matters. Though some labels still operate like this, the new wave of 1960s pop music resulted in more say for the recording artists themselves.

The majority of new rock and pop bands to emerge during the 1960s and 1970s were opposed to the old music industry system and wanted to exert more control over their careers. Many of the new artists wrote their own songs, recorded their music themselves and wanted to have a more equal say in how their records were marketed. As a result, many of today's A & R departments work more closely and co-operatively with their artists.

Once an artist is signed to a record label he or she has to be recorded. These recordings are usually carried out in a specially designed recording studio supervised by a producer. Also helping out is a team of engineers and sometimes arrangers (who arrange accompanying music for artists' songs) or session musicians who provide extra musical accompaniments. It is the producer's job to give the recording artists a distinctive recorded sound that complements their music.

Producers are highly skilled individuals who work with complex studio equipment, recording and blending the various musical sounds made in the studio (and often combining as many as 48 separate music tracks at once). This is often ignored as a creative skill, but top producers can earn a large amount of money for their ability to make the best of a group's sounds, seeing possibilities that the band may not have seen. Some producers even go on to be famous for a particular sound in their own right: for example, the sixties American pop producer Phil Spector, the British producers Stock, Aitken and Waterman, the popular American soul team Jimmy Jam and Terry Lewis or the British producer of Bhangra Rock, Deepack Khazanchi. Top arrangers and session musicians are also much in demand and can add extra quality to an artist's sounds.

New bands like Brother Beyond appear on television shows in order to publicize their records and gain more sales.

Once an artist's music has been recorded it has to be manufactured on record, cassette or CD, packed in covers, sent out to record shops and marketed. Marketing is the process of getting the maximum publicity for a product in order to sell the maximum amount of copies. Record companies market their records by advertising in the press, on commercial radio and (increasingly) on television. The artists publicize their own material by going on concert tours, appearing in pop videos and making guest appearances on radio and television.

Most large record companies have art departments who work out cover designs for records, consult with the recording artists and then arrange photographic sessions and carry out the graphic design. Often these cover designs are co-ordinated with a broader campaign of posters, advertising and displays in record shops. The production of these images is very important since attractive cover design can draw attention to the record itself, whereas an unattractive one can sometimes put people off buying it.

Advertising is an important element in any campaign. The advertising department has a

set sum of money (a budget) to spend on placing adverts for the artist. It has to make sure the money is spent in the most effective way and has to produce appealing adverts and put them in the particular media likely to attract most potential buyers. In Britain, for instance, groups appealing to a younger audience will be advertised in teenage magazines such as *Just Seventeen* and *Smash Hits,* whereas groups with older audiences may be advertised in a variety of publications — national newspapers such as the *Guardian* (on its weekly music page), fashionable magazines such as *The Face* or *City Limits,* or pop papers such as the *New Musical Express* (NME).

Music papers such as the *NME, Melody Maker* and *Smash Hits,* as well as American magazines such as *Rolling Stone* or *Creem,* are very important to the music industry. The stories these magazines run on music and musicians draw valuable attention to new artists. When the music press decides to champion a new artist or band, this can often prove more effective in launching a new artist than advertising itself. Many successful new artists (such as Curiosity Killed The Cat and Terence Trent d'Arby) have become highly successful early in their careers almost entirely through this kind of publicity. However, this route to success can be dangerous. Too much early publicity can raise expectations too high and if the act cannot live up to the expectations publicity can soon work against them, resulting in records being failures right from the start.

The advertising and publicity for new releases is carefully timed by the record companies to create the maximum impact in order to try to place the record in the charts. Once a record sells enough copies in a week to get into the bestseller charts it is guaranteed a place on radio playlists. This means that more people are able to hear it and sales therefore increase. Being in the charts also means that

Above   *Groups like Curiosity Killed the Cat are popular almost as much for their image as for the music they record.*

Below   *Music magazines play a crucial role in setting trends and introducing artists to a wider public.*

radio and television chart shows feature the record, music papers run features on new stars and people begin talking about them (a valuable form of publicity known as 'word of mouth').

The charts are not just a sales chart for the industry, they are a highly successful marketing device in themselves. Indeed, the charts are so important to the success or failure of an individual record that some record companies or artist's managers have in the past tried to 'rig' or 'hype' the charts by making it appear that a record is selling far more copies than it is. The record industry tries hard to prevent obvious attempts to do this, but numerous companies try to get record shops to order large numbers of records in advance of sales, so that individual records will be listed in the charts as quickly as possible.

By the time an artist has reached the top of her or his profession press reviews are less important, since major artists gain a large following who often ignore bad reviews or publicity. Fans often buy new albums or concert tickets simply because the artist has achieved a long standing international status. Artists such

Below *Frankie Goes to Hollywood were controlled by their producers and did not even play on their major international hit 'Relax'.*

Above *Bruce Springsteen is so well established that he needs little publicity to sell out concerts or have hit records.*

In order to control all aspects of his music Prince set up his own record label Paisley Park.

as Bruce Springsteen, Phil Collins and Diana Ross have all reached this position. This is not to say that the record companies do not continue carefully to market new products by established artists, but rather that their job is easier than successfully 'breaking' (making popular) a new act.

Within this overall commercial set-up there are various kinds of relationships between the companies and their artists. Some groups are carefully moulded by the company to produce a sound and an image that the company thinks will be successful with the public. A group like Frankie Goes To Hollywood, is one example; their sound and image were carefully designed by ZTT Records' bosses Trevor Horn and Paul Morley. Established artists such as Prince, The Rolling Stones, Madness and Jefferson Starship have, however, gone to the other extreme and set up their own record labels to avoid outside interference.

Along with the major international companies there are many other companies from medium-sized ones like Virgin and Island Records, through to much smaller specialist labels like Sterns, Rough Trade, 4AD and Rounder Records. Many of these labels concentrate on specialist forms of music whose sales are big enough to attract the major companies. They are often prepared to give recording contracts to new acts with a distinctive new sound that is not yet popular with a mass audience. Many of these labels do the valuable work of developing new acts and helping them break through to a wider public only to have big companies step in and lure them away once they become famous.

Some of these small independent labels achieve enough success to become major operations. These include Def Jam, Virgin, Mute, Stax and Tamla Motown. But whether they achieve international success or not (and most do not), many of these labels are kept going by individuals who have a love for a particular sort of music. It is their efforts that ensure that the record buying public has a wider choice of music rather than the often predictable product put out by most of the major companies.

3 | Pop music radio

Popular music and radio are now closely identified with each other. In Britain two of the BBC's four national channels (Radios One and Two) play a great deal of pop music throughout the day. Across the USA a massive network of stations play different sorts of popular music to cater for the different tastes of their listeners. Though we now take this for granted, the relationship between radio stations, musicians and recording companies has not always been as smooth as it is today.

In the early days of radio, record companies feared that the playing of popular music on radio would decrease record sales (and indeed it did). From 1924 radio stations in Europe and the USA began broadcasting live dance band concerts. In Britain these became social events, with families rolling up their carpets and dancing to live music in their homes. These concerts were also accompanied by another threat to record sales, the first radio programmes where a disc jockey (DJ) would introduce and play a selection of records.

Record companies depend on radio stations for airplay which helps to increase sales.

In the USA in the 1920s and 1930s the most popular form of radio music was that provided by the so-called big bands. These were large groups who featured a brass section and several singers and often performed 'live' on radio from the dance halls and hotel ballrooms where they played for the public. These concerts were, however, expensive for radio stations to record and by the 1940s the stations were increasingly cutting down on concert transmissions and playing more records instead. This development combined with the gradual replacement of live music in bars by jukeboxes meant less work for live musicians. As a result the American Musicians' Union went on strike in 1942 demanding higher pay for recording the records that were depriving them of live work.

In 1941 another industrial dispute had a major effect on the sort of music played on American radio. An organization called ASCAP (the American Society of Composers, Authors and

After establishing herself through live concerts, Ella Fitzgerald became one of the first of a new generation of singers to get radio airplay in the 1940s.

Publishers) demanded that radio stations double the fees paid to composers and songwriters whose music was broadcast on the radio. The radio stations refused and stopped playing all music written by members of the association. Since the majority of established composers and songwriters were in ASCAP, radio stations had to look for talent outside the established music business. But as well as employing new songwriters and composers they also turned to other sorts of music that they had not played before such as blues, country music and jazz. Even though the ASCAP dispute finished after 10 months the new sorts of music continued to be played and the power of the old style of traditional popular music was broken for ever.

In the early days of radio, the BBC would broadcast live concerts by popular bands of the time.

In Britain different influences opened up popular music programming on the radio. During the Second World War it became important to keep up public morale and the BBC played more popular music to respond to this need, introducing shows like 'Music While You Work'. A number of British listeners were also able to listen to even more up-to-date popular music programmes. These were the programmes broadcast by the American Forces Network (the AFN). The AFN was a service intended for American troops in Europe which brought together the most popular programmes from a range of US stations. It was not intended for British audiences, but residents living near US bases could pick up the signals and listen to a range of adventurous American popular music programmes. The war created such a popularity for this lively sort of music that the BBC altered its structure in 1945 to include three separate channels, one of which (the Light Programme) was devoted to popular music and comedy shows.

British radio broadcasting stayed relatively stable for the next 20 years, with the BBC sticking to a style of light entertainment designed to appeal to all age groups. When rock and roll and a new style of pop music became increasingly popular from the late 1950s the BBC was slow to respond, seeming suspicious of the energetic new sounds. By the early 1960s they were increasingly out of step with the young people who formed a large part of their audience. The pop music that young people wanted to hear was simply not being played on the radio.

The BBC eventually introduced a pop music channel in 1967 in response to the popularity of the illegal 'pirate' radio stations. The first British pirate radio station was set up in 1964 by an Irish businessman called Ronan O'Rahilly. The station was called Radio Caroline and was located on a ship in the North Sea which was outside British territorial waters (the area of coastline that belongs to Britain). From this location Radio Caroline beamed an all day service of non-stop pop music that proved massively popular with the young people who tuned in to it. Other pirate radio stations based off the coast were quick to follow Radio Caroline's example. By 1966 the government was seriously concerned about the situation and introduced a parliamentary bill to close down pirate stations. To compensate for this the BBC introduced a pop radio channel of its own called Radio One, and employed a number of leading pirate radio DJs to work on it. Since then over 40 local independent radio stations have been founded in Britain. They are regulated by the Independent Broadcasting Authority (IBA) to ensure the programmes they make are of a high standard.

Above   *Pirate DJ Tony Blackburn was employed by the new BBC Radio One in 1967 in an attempt to attract the same audiences as the pirate radio stations.*

Below   *Pirate station Radio Caroline was massively successful with young listeners in the days before Radio One.*

Radio stations in the USA responded to the introduction of new forms of popular music much faster than the BBC in Britain. Being commercial stations (unlike the BBC which is a non-profit making public service) the stations had to give audiences what they wanted, and when pop music came on to the scene they began to play it immediately. But even with this broadening of policy from the 1960s onwards in both Britain and the USA, it is still difficult for minority music to receive airplay on the major radio channels. Sales of mainstream rock and

Sometimes artists can become popular after someone else has a hit with one of their songs. This happened to Bob Marley.

Community Radio is already well established in countries like Australia. Britain will soon have a network of local community stations.

pop music are boosted by radio plays but many other forms of music do not get the proportion of radic airtime that would enable them to sell as many records as other types of music.

To make matters worse, it often seems that highly inventive forms of music can only become hits if famous recording artists become involved with them — Eric Clapton had a hit with Bob Marley's 'I Shot the Sheriff' before Marley became successful with international audiences. Paul Simon featured leading black South African musicians such as Ladysmith Black Mambazo on his hit album *Graceland* before they gained international recognition. The Beastie Boys got rap music on the same mainstream radio stations who had previously all but ignored rap music.

In Britain, reggae, contemporary soul, and 'alternative' music has suffered on independent record labels especially badly, with the national station Radio One being reluctant to include it on its 'playlist' in anything but special shows broadcast when audience listening figures are low. The playlist system is a way of carefully controlling the choice of records played by the radio and reflects the tastes of the radio broadcasters and what they think their audience should like. Often many of the individuals who choose the music are much older than their audiences and out of touch with popular trends. This has resulted in a situation similar to the 1960s, with a number of unlicensed 'pirate' radio stations being set up to play the sorts of music mostly ignored by national and local radio. British radio is, however, soon to undergo a major change. Government legislation is going to introduce a network of local radio stations run by groups representing local communities. This is likely to result in a far greater range of music being played, and though it is unlikely that pirate broadcasting will disappear altogether, it should mean that those broadcasters who currently have to break the law in order to play their music may be able to do this legally. The greater coverage of different styles of music may also encourage national radio stations to extend their own playlists as well.

4 Pop music and youth culture

Pop music is more complex than it at first seems. On one level it is a business where decisions about records and artists are made on the basis of making the maximum profits. It is also a highly important part of the social and cultural life and experiences of young people.

Pop music is not just about sound; it is also about styles and attitudes that are reflected in patterns of speech, dress and behaviour.

New generations of young people become fans of particular forms of music which stand as a symbol for their experiences. For them, the music becomes more than mere sounds. Particular groups or singers become heroes or heroines to look up to, sex symbols to admire or role models from whom to copy dress styles or behaviour. But this is not just a one-way process. Young people do not just consume pop music, they use it creatively, devising new

Nick Kamen became famous as a model in the Levi 501 advert; he then turned into a pop star and is seen as a symbol of style by record buyers.

dance movements, hair and fashion styles and behaviour patterns.

For young people one of the attractions of new groups and new forms of music is precisely that they are new and different. Young people often feel that their life, experiences and creativity need to be expressed in ways unique to them. When a new singer or group becomes highly popular with young people they are sometimes said to be 'the voice of a generation', expressing the needs, desires and fears of a large group of young people.

Older people often dislike these new styles of music for precisely the same reasons. They find them threatening to their established musical tastes and are suspicious of the attitudes, personalities and cultural backgrounds of both the individuals who play them and the young people who become fans. Parents in particular are often highly critical of new forms of popular music admired by their children, and if the behaviour associated with it is particularly extreme the popular press usually covers it with sensational reports and headlines.

Above The Sun *newspaper covers stories in a sensational way. It gave The Beastie Boys' 1987 UK tour dramatic coverage and headlines.*

Below *The lyrics of Morrissey (The Smiths) are popular for expressing the feelings and experiences of the fans who buy his records.*

But this sort of social outcry is not new. Ever since the early days of rock and roll and jazz there has been opposition to new forms of music and the fans they attract. This has been particularly true in Britain where new forms of American culture have often been seen as threatening to so-called 'traditional' British values.

Indeed, so repetitive is this process that each generation repeats the same old comments to criticize new fashions in music. We have all probably heard older people make remarks about our favourite groups like 'this isn't music,

it's just noise', 'it all sounds the same', 'they can't play their instruments' or 'they don't write songs like they used to'. But it is worth bearing in mind that in the past these comments have been levelled at all sorts of people, from respected jazz musicians such as Duke Ellington and John Coltrane to massively popular pop stars such as Elvis Presley, The Rolling Stones and Bob Marley. These days the generation who

Run DMC and The Beastie Boys have the same tough guy image as previous generations of rock, reggae and soul singers.

Above *For Sex Pistol Sid Vicious the rebel image was not just a pose, but a life style which led to his tragic early death, at the age of twenty-one, by taking an overdose of heroin.*

Above *James Dean was the original teenage rebel who provided the image for a host of stars who followed. His life also came to an early end when he was tragically killed in a car crash.*

grew up with sixties rock groups like The Rolling Stones and The Who now criticize rap groups like The Beastie Boys and Run DMC using exactly the same phrases that older generations used to insult their favourites.

For young people it is often this parental dislike that attracts them to the music. One famous writer went so far as to call early rock and roll music 'the soundtrack for teenage rebellion', and at various times new styles of music have been launched with this rebellious image. The punk rock movement of the late 1970s was a notable example.

In the mid 1970s rock music was going through a very stable and unexciting period. Major rock stars who started their careers in the 1960s had reached the top of their trade and were earning a lot of money, dominating both the charts and the record industry. At the same time a new generation was growing up. This generation could not identify with these rich 'superstars' and their slick and predictable music. They turned instead to new bands whose lyrics and straightforward harsh sound reflected a generation growing up with increased unemployment and the poor conditions of inner-city life. To their followers the punk bands were a powerful symbol of rebellion against the establishment.

The punk image belongs to a long tradition of teenage rebellion. In the 1950s Elvis Presley and James Dean presented rebellious images, then there were the 'Rude Boy' reggae styles of the 1960s and now there is the attitude of 1980s rap stars like The Beastie Boys. Female rebel figures are less overt in the history of pop music (reflecting its continuing tradition of male dominance), but singers as different as Tina

Turner, Siouxsie (and the Banshees), and Madonna, Cyndi Lauper and Janet Jackson have all upset conventions of so-called 'respectable' female behaviour.

This sense of 'threat' to established values is all the more noticeable if the styles and attitudes of a new form of pop music come from minority groups within the community. The popularity of seventies punk music and eighties rap music shares similar roots in the experience of poor or unemployed young people living in inner cities. Both forms of music are particularly

Janet Jackson adopted a tough style, which brought her great chart success as well as many music industry awards.

Pop music can represent the life styles and feelings of ordinary people. Punk music reflected the experiences of the young unemployed.

harsh and do not require great musical training to play — all they need are energy and the capacity to be inventive with what is available.

Both styles invented their own dance forms; Punks devised the violently energetic styles of pogoing and slam dancing, and rap music fans developed the dangerously athletic form known as breakdancing. Their songs are often concerned with images of violence and frustration which sometimes spill over in the behaviour of their fans. These factors have often resulted in concerts being banned or raided by the police and hysterical hate campaigns being run in the tabloid press. Surprisingly, this press hysteria is often highly advantageous to all concerned. Newspapers sell more copies, fans both enjoy the scandal and enjoy defending their favourites, and the record companies keep quiet and appreciate the free publicity, which results in increased record sales.

In many ways it is the audience and fan following of pop music that makes 'pop culture' as a whole. Pop culture is just as much about what people actually do when they go out to a disco, watch a band perform or listen to their radio or record player as it is the making of records themselves. It is these social activities that create the *experience* of pop music and bring about those changes in taste which see some pop stars suddenly fall from fashion but allow others to continue for years. Stars like Adam and the Ants or The Thompson Twins may be massively popular one year but almost totally forgotten the next. Similar artists such as Los Lobos may make the same sort of music for years and then suddenly become fashionable after getting a lucky break like working on a film

Left *Boy George's colourful image has brought him a lot of media attention. Scandalous news stories have always kept him in the public eye.*

Above *USA for Africa and Live Aid showed the power of the music business in influencing world opinion and raising money for charity.*

soundtrack.

It is this factor that makes the pop music industry a far more unpredictable and risky business than selling other commercial products such as chocolates or soap powder. Although many critics still argue that all pop music 'sounds the same', even the expert staff of record companies find it hard to tell which particular group or record will be popular with the public. Record companies often make mistakes and find that even top artists can sometimes make records that do not sell, while other recording artists keep a loyal following for years, whatever the quality of music they put out. It is factors such as these that make pop music the lively, fascinating and complex activity that it is.

31

5 Cinema and video

Over the last 30 years pop music has become a standard ingredient of both cinema and television production. With the rise of promotional pop videos in the late 1970s, this influence has become even more widespread.

While pop videos may be relatively new, the association of popular music and moving images dates back a long way.

Even in the days when films were silent, music was an important part of going to the cinema. Silent films were usually screened with a musical accompaniment provided by a pianist (or even orchestra in big city film theatres). When films with sound (known as 'talkies') were introduced in the USA in the late 1920s, the first to go on general release was a musical called *The Jazz Singer* (1927). This film attracted large

In the 1950s Bill Haley and the Comets starred in Blackboard Jungle, *which proved so sensational that fans rioted and vandalized cinemas.*

audiences and the musical went on to become one of the most popular forms of Hollywood cinema during the 1930s and 1940s. Musicals also caught on in Britain during this period and singing stars like George Formby and Gracie Fields became major celebrities. The Indian film industry also started producing musicals at this time and has continued to do so ever since.

The beginnings of rock and roll in the 1950s gave birth to a whole series of films featuring the new style of music. The majority of these were 'B-movies', films made cheaply and quickly to exploit current tastes and fashions. Most were highly forgettable, but some, such as *Rock Around the Clock* (1956), featured music from leading rock and roll groups such as Bill Haley and the Comets, and succeeded in capturing the imagination of young audiences in both North America and Europe.

With the growth of rock and pop music in the 1960s, more youth-orientated films featuring

The Beatles' film Help *set the pattern for a whole range of rock movies and TV shows, such as The Monkees.*

music followed, including a series of American 'Beach Movies' with titles like *Beach Party* and *Bikini Beach*. But perhaps the biggest influence on film and television pop coverage was the film of the Beatles directed by Richard Lester in 1964, called *A Hard Day's Night*. The film was a lively and heavily fictionalized account of the life of the band, mixing songs, comedy and chase sequences in an energetic style which appealed to its young audiences. The follow-up, *Help!* (1965), continued this successful formula and was so popular that it led American director Bob Rafelson to make a similar style television series based around a specially created group called the Monkees. This also proved a success with audiences and is still repeated on television today.

By the late 1960s and early 1970s, pop music was beginning to take itself more seriously and a new type of music film was established. This was the concert film – a feature-length documentary recording the music and general atmosphere of the large open air rock festivals which were being held all over the USA at the time. The most famous of these films were *Monterey Pop* (1968), *Woodstock* (1970) and *Gimme Shelter* (1971). Following this example, a number of famous bands also made feature-length films based around their own concerts, such as Pink Floyd's film *Live At Pompeii* (1971) Led Zeppelin's *The Song Remains The Same* (1976) or ABBA's *The Movie* (1977).

These films did much to promote the careers of individual bands and artists and enabled them to be seen in areas where they did not go on tour. It was not until the late 1970s that the record companies came up with a way of using film and video material to boost the sales of particular records. This came with the introduction of pop videos.

The idea of having a brief film clip to promote a record or artist went back to the 1930s when clips of jazz or rhythm and blues tunes by artists

The Rolling Stones appeared in the film Gimme Shelter *enabling their fans all around the world to see footage of them live in concert.*

such as Duke Ellington or Big Joe Turner were made to be shown in bars in the USA. These were however, intended only for minority audiences and it was not until television began to feature pop music that the direct marketing link between the two became clearly apparent.

In the 1960s, television pop shows often included snippets of film, either provided by the artists or made by the stations to accompany individual records. Groups such as the Beatles and the Rolling Stones often took care and attention over these film clips, but it was not until the late 1970s that the pop promotional video industry really became important. In Britain in 1976 an up-and-coming rock group called Queen released a single called 'Bohemian Rhapsody'. The record was more than a minute longer than the standard radio play length and the company (EMI Records) decided to make a special promotional clip to show on television in order to boost sales. When the clip appeared on the BBC chart show Top of the Pops, it proved so popular with audiences that sales of the

Queen made a video for their single Bohemian Rhapsody. *It was so popular that record sales increased substantially.*

record shot up due to the success of the promotional video itself. With this the industry realized that well-made pop videos could increase record sales. Many record companies went on to finance ambitious videos for songs such as the Boomtown Rats 'I Don't Like Mondays' or Ultravox's 'Vienna', which helped push the records to the top of the charts.

In Britain, which has only one national pop channel (Radio One), national radio exposure for new artists is very limited. There are also only a small number of pop programmes broadcast on the four national television channels. Because of this, the individual screening of a pop video on a television show such as Top of the Pops can have a significant effect on the national sales of the record. Consequently pop video production took off in Britain more quickly than it did in countries such

as the USA where no one show had such power. It was not until 1982, with the introduction of the US cable channel MTV (Music Television), that US record companies began to realize the marketing advantages of video.

In the first twelve months of MTV, few leading American recording artists made videos to accompany their current singles and the channel had to rely on a lot of British-produced pop videos to fill its airtime. This shortage of material led it to include videos by British bands who had little or no reputation in the USA. The effect of this television exposure was to boost the groups' record sales and establish new bands like Ultravox and Adam Ant in the USA without the usual expensive combination of lengthy national tours and widespread advertising campaigns.

Above *Adam Ant was already successful in Britain and became highly popular in the USA after his videos were shown on MTV.*

Pop videos were originally made for television as a form of promotion, but are now widely sold alongside records, cassettes and compact discs.

American record companies soon saw that they were missing out on a commercial opportunity and began to make promotional videos for their big stars. The result was that from 1983 many of the lesser known acts who had appeared on MTV in the early years no longer had the same chance of exposure. These days MTV simply has the effect of boosting major artists' sales even further and actually preventing new acts from getting on television.

The success of pop videos on television has also resulted in them being made available for sale on video cassette. Although groups such as Blondie have released full-length video versions of their own LPs, most promotional videos for hit singles have been made available in compilation packages along with videos

Michael Jackson has projected both his image and his music to wider audiences by making promotional videos like Thriller *which have themselves sold in large amounts.*

made by other groups. Another form of popular video release has been the concert video where one band's live performance is released on video like a live album. The most successful long-playing promotional release to date has been the documentary tape The Making of Michael Jackson's Thriller, which combines Jackson's highly atmospheric Thriller video (directed by John Landis) with a short account of how it was made. This video has now sold almost one million copies worldwide (all of which have in turn promoted Michael Jackson's original album).

Though many critics have dismissed pop videos as boring, clichéd and repetitive, others have seen them as a new exciting form of media which gives talented video makers the opportunity to be creative in a way they could not be in film or television. Artists such as Madonna have worked with a number of different directors to produce a series of distinctly original videos for singles such as 'True Blue' and 'Papa Don't Preach', which make highly inventive use of choreography, visual style and the star's own personal image. Other musicians such as Kate Bush have learnt from their experience of working with video directors and gone on to direct their own. David Byrne from the American group Talking Heads has not only directed a prize-winning video for his group (the promotional video for their 'Road to Nowhere' single), but has also gone on to direct a major film called *True Stories* (1986).

Madonna has become famous for making good quality and entertaining videos that have helped promote her songs and sell more records.

The distinctive fast pace and vivid visual style of pop videos have also influenced television and cinema production itself. A number of television programmes have attempted to incorporate aspects of pop video styles into their own format. The detective series *Miami Vice* is the most obvious example of this, mixing action sequences accompanied by rock music with glamorous pop video style action and guest appearances by well-known pop stars: a mixture which lives up to the original idea behind the series — an 'MTV cop show'. Other more inventive television programmes such as *Moonlighting* have also drawn on aspects of pop video style to produce their own creative approach to television drama.

Cinema has also become increasingly aware of the appeal of pop video style sequences. New films are now often released along with a promotional video for a song from the film's soundtrack. These videos usually mix clips of the group performing the song and clips of the film itself. This dual release has major benefits for all concerned. A successful song attracts audiences to the film it appears in while a successful film increases the popularity of the song and group. The film and title track promotional video of Ivan Reitman's *Ghostbusters* (1984) was a notable early example of this, but the practice is now almost standard for major film releases. Pop videos have also had an influence on the style of the films themselves. Recent movies such as *Beverly Hills Cop* (1985), *Top Gun* (1986) and *Who's That Girl?* (1987) all feature lengthy sequences that borrow heavily from the distinctive visual styles and editing of pop videos.

Whatever your opinion of the worth of pop videos, they are a major influence on film and television in the 1980s and are likely to be remembered as one of the decade's most original forms of media production.

As well as being a successful rock star, Tina Turner has starred in the film Mad Max 3.

6 Future sounds

In its 100 years of existence the recording industry has been through several periods of rapid technological change. These periods have often resulted in marked changes in patterns of music listening which have appeared to threaten the livelihood of musicians and the profits of record companies. With the rapid development and diversification of technology over the last 10 years these pressures have become increasingly evident. The introduction of the audio-cassette and CD have already had an effect, but in the future it is likely that more far-reaching changes will take place.

Recording technology is continually changing; records and cassettes have been replaced by the compact disc, with its higher quality reproduction and sturdier format.

Pop fans will always support their favourite artist with enthusiasm. These fans wait outside a record company to see their heroes or maybe even get their autographs.

Some of these changes could involve what is known as 'new delivery systems'. A delivery system is simply a way of getting recorded music from one place to another. Tapes and discs are material means of delivering sounds from the manufacturer to the customer, but in the future it seems that delivery systems might increasingly be electronic.

The full range of musical sounds can now be stored as electronic data in computers. By linking up computer data banks to people's homes and public places, it will be technically possible in the future for music to be sent from one place to another in the form of a signal. Customers would then be able to choose the music they want to hear and receive it electronically without having to leave their house or buy any material object. The

telephone 'dial a disc' services now on offer are an early version of this but are very restricted in terms of both the range they offer and the quality of sound that can be received over a telephone line.

This system would have advantages. You would no longer need to go out to buy records or cassettes, and you would not have to find space to store them. Since the music would be stored electronically at a central data base there would also be no danger of damaging the records themselves and no danger of them wearing out.

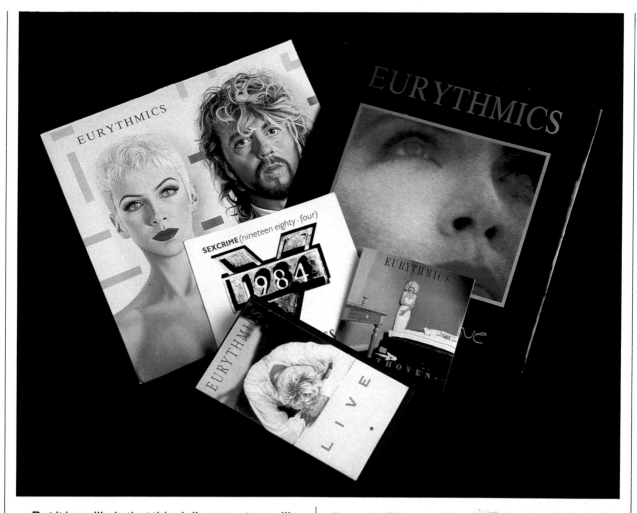

But it is unlikely that this delivery system will replace records, cassettes and CDs completely. One of the pleasures of buying records is to go out to music shops and look through racks of carefully designed record and cassette sleeves before purchasing. Another pleasure is collecting records and having them as physical objects that can be stored at home. Although new computerized delivery systems may present screen graphics in place of record sleeve designs and may offer information sheets that can be printed off on a home computer printer, the attraction of traditional record and cassette packaging is not likely to end.

If this system were ever to be developed on a large scale it would affect the popularity of national radio music broadcasting, since it is likely that it would offer continually updated 'packages' of music for people with different tastes. These audiences would then be able to

Records, CDs, cassettes and videos are designed to be appealing items to collect in their own right.

George Michael started his career in the pop group Wham! but has moved on to even greater success as a solo artist.

select the sort of music programmes they like rather than having to listen to a particular radio DJ who just happens to be on. One drawback of this is that whereas radio is provided free to those owning a radio set, data-delivered music services are likely to be charged to customers at a standard rate per minute — the more you listen to, the more you pay.

As well as new delivery systems, the rapidly developing field of interactive computer technology is likely to bring together the different activities of playing your own musical instruments and listening to recorded music.

There is already a device on sale in Japan called the *karaoke* which enables you to record your voice over the backing track of a well-known song, and new technology is likely to take this idea several stages further. In the not-too-distant future it should be possible to obtain access to a digital recording of one of your favourite pieces of music and alter it electronically, taking individual instruments or voices out and adding new ones (such as your own), or changing the tempo or key of the music to suit yourself.

While it is very difficult to predict the actual types of music that will become popular in the future, it is certain that the music of the last 30 years will prove far longer-lived than its critics first suggested. Audiences tend to remain attached to the style of music that they grew up with, so that rock and roll, Tamla Motown and 1980s records will probably still be played in 25 years' time.

New stars continually emerge. Bros is made up of three teenage boys with good looks and fashionable clothes who appeal to young audiences.

Above *Whitney Houston has sold millions of records and received many awards. She is likely to be popular for many years to come.*

The Pet Shop Boys. Neil Tennant (left) and Chris Lowe (right) use the latest electronic synthesisers and production technology when in the recording studio to give their records an up to date sound.

Glossary

A & R department The department of a record company which looks after the artists on its label and finds new acts.

Arranger the person who works out extra musical accompaniments for a recording artist or performer.

CD A Compact Disc – a small plastic disc played by a special sort of record player which uses a laser instead of a needle.

Format The size, shape and type of an object (eg a record, cassette or CD).

Marketing The process of getting as much publicity for a product (eg a record) in order to sell as many copies as possible.

Phonograph An early type of record player.

Pirate A radio station that broadcasts illegally (without a licence).

Playlist The list of records that are played by radio stations.

Producer An individual who supervises the recording of a record and creates a distinctive sound for it.

Product Anything produced by a business which is sold for profit.

Royalty A small sum of money paid to a recording artist, songwriter (or occasionally producer) which is a percentage of the value of each copy of a record that has been sold.

Session musician A musician who plays with the recording artist at a recording session.

Further Information

For further information on the subjects covered in this book, please contact the following organizations:

ASCAP – American Society of Composers, Authors & Publishers
1 Lincoln Plaza, New York, NY 10023, USA
AMES – Association of Media Education in Scotland
The Scottish Curriculum Development Centre, Moray House College of Education, Holyrood Road, Edinburgh, EH8 8AQ, Scotland
APRS – Association of Professional Recording Studios, 23 Chestnut Avenue, Chorleywood, Herts, WD3 4HA, UK
ATOM – Australian Association of Teachers of Media
PO Box 222, Carlton South, Victoria 3053, Australia
BMIC – British Music Information Centre
10 Stratford Place, London, W1N 9AE, UK
BPI – British Phonographic Industry
4th Floor, Roxburghe House, 273/287 Regent Street, London, W1R 7PB, UK
IFPVP – International Federation of Phonogram and Videogram Producers, 54 Regent Street, London, W1R 5PJ, UK
MRIB – Media Research and Information Bureau
12 Manchester Mews, London, W1M 5PJ, UK
NARAS – National Academy of Recording Arts and Sciences, 303 North Gen Oaks Boulevard, Suite 140, Burbank, CA 91502, USA
RIAA – Recording Industry Association of America
888 Seventh Avenue, New York, NY 10106, USA

Further Reading

J. Burchill and T. Parsons *The Boy Looked at Johnny* (Pluto, 1978)

I. Chambers *Popular Culture — The Metropolitan Experience* (Methuen, 1986)

L. Ferrari and C. James *Wham Teaching Pack* (BFI, 1988)

M. Haralambos *Right On: From Blues to Soul in Black America* (Edison, 1974)

T. Palmer *All You Need is Love* (Futura, 1977)

S. Steward and S. Garratt *Signed, Sealed and Delivered: True Life Stories of Women in Pop* (Pluto, 1984)

Students might also refer to issues of magazines such as The *NME (New Musical Express)*, *The Face*, *Smash Hits*, and *Rolling Stone* which often carry interesting and well researched articles on a range of popular music and music-related topics.

Picture acknowledgements
The author and publishers would like to thank the following for allowing their illustrations to be reproduced in this book:
BBC (Hulton Picture Library) 6; Camera Press 53; Cassidy 23; CBS (Records) 44; London Features International 31; Popperfoto 21 (bottom); Duncan Raban (All-Action) *cover*, 10 (both), 14, 15 (top), 16 (top), 16 (bottom), 17, 26, 28, 35, 36 (top), 38, 39, 41, 44 (top); David Redfern 4, 7 (top), 8, 9, 13, 19, 21 (top), 22, 24 25 (bottom), 30, 32, 34, 43; Rex Features 12, 37; Topham Picture Library 20, 27 (left); Wayland Picture Library 5, 7 (bottom), 11, 15 (bottom), 18, 25 (top), 27, 29, 36 (bottom), 40, 42. (With thanks to Tony Gregory for his professional advice.).

Index

figures in **bold** refer to illustrations